To Veroni
with Lou

MW00414327

Dedicated to my granddaughter Ava

with the hope that someday she'll read it.

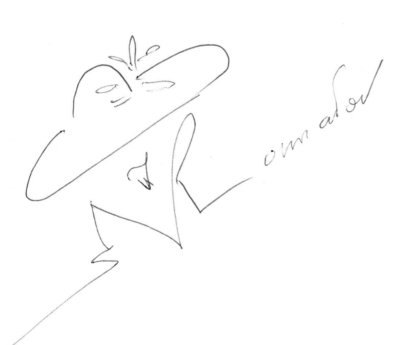

Table of Content

INTRODUCTION
By MaryLois Altman

After decades of sharing her talents with Hollywood, Shelley Komarov has gathered up her silks, satins, gold threads, lace and buttons and built her own fashion line. She has taken her Master's degree, dogged determination, skillful eye from years of training and her flair for all of it and gone even further in her life long career of making clothes.

An understatement to say the least, for this woman with humble fashion roots whose talent and experience has gifted not only those in the land of dreams, but also the average woman who can now own one of Shelley's pieces available to her through Komarov, Inc.

The recipient of numerous awards beyond her Emmys, Shelley has graced a famous fashion house, the ballet, television and feature film sets with her skills for decades. Her career runs the gamut. Throughout the years she has worked with, and literally dressed, such stars as Halle Berry, Julianna Margulies, Nicole Kidman, Jack Lemmon, George C. Scott, Charles Bronson, Patrick Swayze, Richard Dreyfuss, George Clooney, Loretta Young, Vanessa Redgrave and Matthew McConaughey.

Through it all, it has been her utter sense of self, of who she is and who she isn't, of what she believes and of what works for her that has allowed her to succeed. And now with her clothing line, she is able to help other women gain this sense for themselves, to help them be the movie stars of their own life.

Chapter One
Early Years

∞ ∞ ∞ ∞

"Underneath the folds of many of Hollywood's exquisite costumes lies the heart of five year

old Shelley Komarov who dreamed of a career in fashion.

Looking back over her life following this dream, as an award winning Hollywood film, television and theater Costume Designer and Entrepreneur, it is hard to imagine her own wardrobe roots."

MaryLois Altmann

I was born in the former Soviet Union during the Cold War and for as long as I can remember, from about age five or six, I wanted to become a designer. I didn't know exactly what kind, but I knew I wanted to make clothes. I loved everything about them. Unfortunately, it wasn't easy to be a fashionista in Russia at that time because there weren't a lot of design choices. Our resources, especially fashion options, were very limited, but looking good was critical.

My school uniform and shoes were custom made by a seamstress and a cobbler. With very few choices in fabric, I rarely had more than one dress for going out socially. But, because I was raised with a sense of pride in my appearance, I focused on making statements with my clothing and being stylish, even with what little I had to work with. My girlfriends and I couldn't run out to buy what was "in" at "Forever 21" or similar stores the way young girls can today, so to put together outfits, we had to be creative.

Even in this world of meager choices, everyone paid attention to how they looked, trying extremely hard to appear well groomed. Selections were sparse and there wasn't access to Western styles or even fashion magazines. While to the outside world the stereotypical Soviet woman's dress would have been considered drab, we all did the best we could. It was always important to look nice with whatever we had access to. There was an inherent sense of dignity in looking good.

Shopping as we know it wasn't an option then, making supplies inadequate. But since we didn't have alternatives, we learned to appreciate what we had, to value each piece. There was an overall respect for every article in our wardrobe. Things weren't expendable as they are today. I can remember learning how to fix runs in my nylon stockings. The good ones were from East Germany and very expensive, so when someone gave me a hook as a present, I learned how to use it to repair them. By stretching the nylon over an empty glass and working on runs with the little hook, I was able to wear them again.

It's hard to imagine having to do that today, unheard of really, but at that time we couldn't afford to throw away stockings. We never knew when we might be able to get new ones. We learned to mend holes or burns in cloth and to do alterations, changing sizes from large to small or even from small to large by letting out fabrics. Our pieces were made to last and we paid attention to every detail that went into making them. We took care of them. You couldn't change your outfit on a whim the way you can today. You had to value and appreciate whatever you had and carefully maintain it.

My early experiences helped me in my future professional life. An example of this was during one of my first films as a Hollywood costume designer. It was a murder story, *Murder: By Reason of Insanity,* with Candice Bergen and a German actor named Jurgen Prochnow. Jurgen had to be dressed for an action scene in a shirt that was destroyed during the violent takes. Take after take required shirt after shirt, but we hadn't prepared enough for that.

The year was 1984 and the events in the film were supposedly taking place in the early 1970s, so the wardrobe style was dated. We needed another four or five shirts, but it wasn't as if we could go and buy replacements in a store as fashions had changed dramatically in more than a decade. We were facing a potentially serious wardrobe problem.

As a solution, I cut the back of the shirt off. From that piece of fabric I was able to make five collars, dickeys, and cuffs. Luckily, the actor was wearing a jacket over the shirt, so what I had made were the only parts of the shirt that could be seen on the screen. Everybody thought it was brilliant. For me, it was simply revisiting my past: when you had a nice shirt and the collar and cuffs become worn out, you flipped them and continued wearing them.

Looking back, my desire for working with clothes was always there. It was a thread throughout my life. With a true gift for making dresses and creating flower accessories, I was often seen doing so when I was young. I absolutely loved making clothes. However, the idea of going into a career in fashion didn't seem like an option. My parents were against it because they felt it would be very difficult to find a job in this arena. I actually got a Master's degree in economics, but never worked a day in that field. As fate would have it, I went into the world of fashion after all.

At twenty-one years old, I was invited to work as an assistant at *Leningrad Fashion House*, one of the most prestigious fashion houses in the nation. I was very lucky to have this opportunity because Tatiana (Tanya), the woman I worked under, was a famous designer at that time who had studied under Christian Dior in Paris. As part of the country's effort to be fashion forward, Russia had sent her at great expense to learn from Dior. I was blessed because she passed these lessons along to me.

While I worked with her, beyond making clothing for party officials and celebrities, Tanya was working on a very special collection which would be shown around the world. It would be based on centuries old costumes that had been worn by former Russian imperials such as Elizabeth and Catherine the Great. Price and time would not be an object in making these creations and since pay was so minimal in the country, months could be spent on one dress.

One of my first assignments was to research the embroidery and other embellishments from the vast collection of these invaluable garments worn by royalty which were housed at *The State Hermitage Museum*, one of the finest art museums in the world. My job was to go to *Hermitage* and study the rich collections there while educating myself about the history of each piece. Every one of them was truly a work of art. I had to make drawings of the fabric's embroideries and determine ways to adapt them to our collection.

During my studies I learned that throughout Empress Elizabeth's reign, her gowns numbered over fifteen thousand and that she never wore the same dress twice. Historian Mikhail Shcherbatov describes her as having been "arrayed in cloth of gold." It was absolutely true from looking at her dresses. "The richness and splendour of the Russian Court exceed the most extravagant descriptions ... the luxurious and brilliant apparel is decorated with an abundance of precious stones and is much more splendid than at any other European court," quotes the Hermitage Museum's website today.

For two years I researched there, worked at Leningrad Fashion House and attended classes at the major art school of Leningrad, *Repin Academy of Arts*. I continued tirelessly to figure out how to repeat this incredible handiwork myself and to adapt it to the pieces we were creating. I pored over gowns of velvet, brocade, silk and chiffon. Gowns which were adorned with gold and silver threads, embroideries, silk, colored glass and intricate beading. It was incredible. I made drawing after drawing of what I saw in my efforts to learn to reproduce these complicated Venetian laces and silk stitch embroideries. Once I taught myself, I was able to teach others how to replicate them. Every day, after doing my investigations, I would return to the fashion house and show our embroiderers the things I had mastered. Then, together we would add the embellishments into what we were making. The experience was incredible. It served me enormously later on in Hollywood when I was working on period films. Interestingly, all of my Emmys were received for these type of movies.

During my time at the *Leningrad Fashion House,* I had access to their rich library which included an incredibly comprehensive collection of worldwide fashion magazines. These were not available anywhere else in the Soviet Union. The access I had to this collection was incredibly helpful to me.

When it came to fashion, especially shows, Russia wanted to demonstrate to the West, "We can do it too." In the 1970s, when *Leningrad Fashion House* revealed their collections in Paris, they were met with rave reviews. Everyone wanted something from there, but the availability was very limited and only for the elite few. What we worked on was largely for celebrities and wives of the Party officials. The kinds of ornamentations we were doing weren't being made in the West or elsewhere, because it was so labor intensive.

These collections, the fabulous pieces I was part of creating, required intense work over many months. Each one required enormous amounts of time and energy. Because of this, when Tanya gifted me with a special dress a few times I was incredibly appreciative. I knew how difficult it had been for her to find time to make it and the great amount of effort she'd put in. The impact these gifts had on me has never left me.

While we worked at Leningrad, we were supplied with everything we could possibly need to create spectacular pieces and fashion works of art. We has access to whatever may be required. But, ironically, the average citizen couldn't get any of it. I remember saving simple scraps from work to give to my dressmaker friend as a treat. There was no way she could get these on her own, outside of the Fashion House.

I couldn't help but notice the difference between "us at work" and "them at home" as to what supplies were available.

What the party elite could get and what the average citizen could, had nothing in common. It was truly eye opening.

Over time, I'd continued to be exposed to what was going on in the country politically and economically. What I witnessed helped me gain an understanding of the disparity between the words and the deeds of those who ruled the country. To quote George Orwell, "*some pigs were more equal than others*" in that presumably egalitarian 'classless' society. The atmosphere of lies projected by the state propaganda, combined with repressions for those who dared to think differently was the catalyst in making changes. By then I had married my husband Boris and my son Dimitri was born. Together, in 1978, we came to the United States as political refugees and settled in Northern California.

The transition to life in California was not easy. Boris got a grant at Stanford and I was doing work for various boutiques. Later, we moved to Los Angeles and I worked in an art gallery and taught some classes at Otis Parsons. They actually *grabbed* me to teach there, because at that time no one else knew how to design in a way that adapted for the beadings and embellishments I had mastered back in Russia.

My introduction to Hollywood happened some time later through a friend. When NBC decided to make the miniseries *Peter the Great,* my friend Andrei

Konchalovsky, a Russian director, recommended me to work on the costumes. He told the producer about my Russian roots and extensive experience and I was hired. I worked on this project for a year and a half.

Later, NBC decided to do a co-production with the Soviet Union and shoot the film in Moscow and Leningrad (now St. Petersburg). Not surprisingly, because I was a political refugee, the Soviets were not willing to open a visa for me, so work on the costumes was continued by a designer in Russia. Nevertheless, the experience was tremendous and the miniseries and its costumes won an Emmy.

Throughout my Hollywood career I received four more Emmy nominations and three wins for my work. The awards were for: *Kennedys of Massachusetts, Sinatra,* and *Introducing Dorothy Dandridge.* The miniseries *A Woman Named Jackie* was nominated but didn't win.

Right after finishing *A Woman Named Jackie,* I experienced a truly exciting moment. We had just finished it and I was starting work on *Sinatra* when my assistant came into a meeting to tell me about a phone call. *"Chanel is on the phone,"* she said. *"They'd like to speak to you."* Thinking it was probably a product placement survey, I told her to take a message.

When I called the number back later, it turned out to have been Karl Lagerfeld himself trying to reach me earlier. His assistant answered my call, *"Mrs. Komarov, Mr. Lagerfeld has already gone, but he was calling you to compliment your work on the clothes for 'A Woman Named Jackie."*

I will never forget the feeling I had at that moment holding the phone in my hands. I was terribly disappointed that I hadn't taken that other phone call, but I will always remember the absolute realization at the same time, *"I am a designer!"*

Chapter Two
My World Today

∞ ∞ ∞ ∞

"And now I'm just trying to change the world,

one sequin at a time."

Lady Gaga

A t this point, I would like to say a few words about my company, *Komarov, Inc.*, because its philosophy reflects the ideas that inspired me to write this book. *Komarov, Inc.* is a clothing line I developed along with my son Dimitri and his friend Dima Liberman. Specifically designed for fashionable women on the go like myself, its pieces are all about today's cosmopolitan life style. They are meant to work well within a hectic schedule.

Our company creates items that are individualized and made for women of every age. They flow gracefully and are not only flattering, but extremely soft and comfortable to wear. A Komarov piece needs no ironing or steaming and will look lovely within the course of your day/evening in whatever you do and wherever you go.

In developing our company, I drew from years of experience as a costume designer. With so much time spent traveling, I saw how difficult it was to maintain a wardrobe on the go. Clothes coming out of a suitcase often looked exactly as if they had just come out of one. I wanted to create pieces that could be taken out of the valise looking just as pristine as they had gone in. Pieces that could hold their shape with little effort and that were easy to pack and wear. I also wanted to have options that were forgiving to an older figure, because I feel that women can be gorgeous at any age and want to help them feel that way.

Our company uses a signature pleating that honors women's shapes. Not only does it help maintain the clothing's integrity, but it allows for a better fit and conformity to your body naturally, without the need for many alterations. The cut of each piece serves to accentuate the woman wearing it. Whichever selection from our collections you wear, it will be casual, sexy or fun depending on the mood you are wearing it with.

The clothes in our collections are ideal for today's woman, whatever your status. They are for someone who wants to look great through it all. And although I have retired from Hollywood, I can still relate to having a busy lifestyle and wanting to be beautifully attired in the midst of it. To even think of myself as retired is laughable, but yes, I guess I am, at least from one career. Today my days are focused on another career, my line of clothing. Suffice it to say that keeping up with it is more than a full time job.

My schedule is not the same as it was working on films, but it is still hectic in a different way. Maintaining our business in today's fashion world requires a great deal of time and energy and although I am a fashion designer, I actually don't have to spend much time on my wardrobe. I rely regularly on the pieces we make.

My ideas and inspiration for creating *Komarov's* pieces come from many places. While traveling - and I travel a lot - I am always interested in how people dress in different places and I often draw creative ideas from what I see. I try to determine what is important for them in making their choices and I gather information from my observations. I am also regularly inspired by what I see in nature.

I remember visiting the bird sanctuary in Brazil during my years of traveling. The color combinations of the exotic birds there was astonishing and it became a great influence for me in making our next collection after getting back home. During another trip, a visit to Paris, I noticed a painting in a gallery window on Place des Vosges. It depicted the facade of a building in many different shades of purple, blue and terracotta. As I looked at the painting, it struck me what a perfect color combination I was seeing and I was to use those together later in my designs. No matter where I am, whatever city or country, my love for texture with its depth of different shades is always with me.

I strongly believe that my cultural roots impact my designs. I was born in a seaport of the Black Sea (a part of the Mediterranean Basin), grew up in St. Petersburg and have lived most of my adult life in California. I feel like I am a true hybrid of multiple cultures and places and that my work reflects a bit of all of them.

I also see the impact that cultural roots have on other designers and how they serve to inspire me. The Italians' sense of color and their beautiful textiles becomes easier to understand when you travel there and visit their surroundings. Beautiful villages in Italy, such as Cinque Terra and Positano, are stuck like bird nests on the sides of mountains. Amazing shades of blue, orange, pink, and purple are washed with sea salt and are captured in some of their collections. In others, you can sense their love of flowers, such as what can be seen in the gardens of Lake Como or Lake Maggiore.

The art of German engineering seems to express itself perfectly in the precise tailoring and simplicity of the minimalistic designs of Jil Sander.

Japanese deconstruction designers such as Yamamotto, Comme des Garçon and Issey Miyake very possibly draw inspiration for their work from the sense of complete order and harmony in Nature. Within Ikebana and Japanese gardens, every stone and branch has a special meaning, so perhaps they deconstruct to recreate a new order.

With designers I admire, I often feel that their work has stemmed from an extension of their background and experiences. If I were to choose one in particular that had a great creative impact on me, it would be the brilliant Issey Miyake. In my opinion, each item he has ever created has been a work of art, a piece of sculpture. I have always been enthralled by his prowess, but could never personally fit into any of his pieces. My body is not small and flat, which is the shape he caters to.

In honoring him as my source of inspiration, I found his work very masterful, but I also knew that in my collection I wanted something curve friendly. Not only didn't I fit into his clothes, but I was not aware of many people who could. So, I focused on improving his designs, not aesthetically or conceptually of course, but technologically. Our company set out to build special machines to create what we wanted. We were successful with our unique system and today we have engineers in house who maintain them.

Over the years, through all my travels and my appreciation for other countries and cultures, I have learned that you can change, develop and adapt your taste to new environments that you are exposed to, but your roots stay with you and remain to play an important part in your creations. Because of this it can sometimes be difficult for any foreign brand to find an appeal in a particular culture.

An example of this was in the 1980s when I worked with Loretta Young, one of Hollywood's greats who was famous for her fashion statements. In one of the films I made with her, Loretta was playing the role of Deana Vreeland, editor of *Vogue* magazine. Her role required a great deal of clothing changes. I offered her some pieces of Ungaro, a French designer famous at that time. Some of his pieces had a lot of ruffles. Loretta looked at them and told me they reminded her of a high end bordello. In reality, his inspiration for those pieces had probably come from the French courtesans, those femme du monde and demi-monde.

Today, whether drawing ideas in my travels or at home, I am very busy. I have a beautiful family and great friends. I enjoy visiting museums, art shows, theater, music and the ballet. And for every minute of all of it, I am grateful. I actually believe it is this gratitude that has helped me to achieve and maintain the success that I have.

I always remember how hard I worked and how much I've had to learn to get here. I think of all the lessons along the way and from the early days with limited fashion choices to today's limitless possibility, I appreciate it all. I feel fortunate that my company is able to create its own fabrics today and that I have tools at my fingertips to consistently afford other women the opportunity to look and feel gorgeous in what we offer them.

I believe that wherever you are or whatever country you are in, when you wear *Komarov* pieces, there is a sense of grace, of ease and effortlessness that comes across. What I know from years as a designer is that this casual air can only come from absolute surety and confidence in their production. Quality shines through always. Not only do we have it in our collections but you can feel it when you wear them.

It's exciting to be a woman comfortable in her career and her skin at this point of my life and my goal is to encourage other women to feel the same way. With our dresses and casual wear, we offer opportunities for everyone to feel beautiful and to feel that way with ease. My philosophy is to make you see how gorgeous you are no matter what your age or size and to inspire you not only to feel it but to live it.

Chapter Three
Know Thyself

Be the Star of Your Own Life

∞ ∞ ∞ ∞

"The thing that is really hard, and really amazing, is giving up on perfect and beginning the work of becoming yourself."

Anna Quindlen

In a world where the media seems to speak to women's flaws, I like to call on your strengths. In putting together your unique style, I encourage you to honor your strong points and to accept your gifts with grace. Get to know yourself and be excited about what you have, rather than focusing on what you think you don't. Consider your unique and precious assets and be willing to work with them, instead of against them.

Begin to select fashions that are right for you, that complement you, instead of the ones you think everyone else is wearing. My message is for you to become "The movie star of your own life!" And in doing so, remember that you can be elegant no matter what your shape or size.

Glamour has nothing to do with a number, but everything to do with how you wear what is right for you. A size sixteen is just a piece of clothing and not the person. Someone who wears this size may look gorgeous in an outfit that a size two could never sport and vice versa. The secret is to be willing to try different things in an effort to get to know *you*. Toss out fashion ideas that are not the best ones for you and replace them with ones that are. Knowing what you can wear and what you can't and not taking it personally, sets the stage for your success. Not being able to wear something well doesn't mean you are flawed, it just means it isn't the best choice for you.

Every one of you has a right and wrong style, even the most famous Hollywood stars. Having worked closely with famous actresses for many years, I can absolutely tell you that there is no flawless body or perfect person. It simply doesn't exist. When I was fitting an actress for a wardrobe, we often tried hundreds of styles before deciding on one. If she was working with the hairdresser on set for a color change or a new look, they'd try several before one got the green light. Style experts often work for weeks coming up with an exact style or hue for an outfit, tossing out one after another before finding what is right, but since the average person doesn't see this part, how would you know?

Bear in mind that what you see when you look at a movie star or famous person you admire will be the style choice that was made after all the other choices were rejected, the one that creates the magical look that appears on the stage or screen or in the magazine. Don't get caught up in the idea that what you see as effortless elegance wasn't put together after many trials.

It is critical to remember: There is no such thing as the "ideal" woman or the one that looks perfect in everything. We all have parts of ourselves that we wish were different. We each have styles, colors, shades and tones that are not right for us. Then again, and this is where I like to focus, we each have styles, colors, shades and tones that are.

When you see the most beautiful actresses, the ones who are the epitome of gorgeous, keep in mind that they have the help of a team of fashion consultants, costume designers, stylists, makeup artists and hairdressers that worked to "put them together." Take it from me, I was one of them. Looking at photos or screen shots, remember that hundreds of options didn't work before one did.

In visualizing and then creating your own fashion statement, the trick is to be willing to let go of what doesn't feel right for you and focus on what does and to do so with grace. That is how you will achieve your own elegance. That is what it is all about.

Finding your best, instead of focusing on what you feel is your worst, helps you to get in touch with unique and wonderful you. That is the first step to achieving star quality. You have to rehearse, sometimes over and over, and practice your "lines" in the movie of your life. Be courageous enough to do your outfits over, even if that means acting out "take after take" to get to your own opening night style. And just because you don't have makeup and wardrobe departments at your disposal, you still can be a star. You still can shine.

Look in the mirror. That's where all of your efforts should begin. Look in there and find you. Others can make suggestions, but no-one else can absolutely tell you what is right for you. That's the trick, so pay attention. It has nothing to do with what is in season. It doesn't matter what the neckline of the moment is.

If "V" necks are in and you have a round face and large breasts, go for it! But, if your face is thin and long, a scoop neck may be much better. If your shoulders are small, thin slip straps can be great on you. If they are wide, you may want to go with a bit more sleeve and some décolletage. If you are sensitive about cleavage or lack thereof, you may want to opt for something else entirely.

Find what's right for the season of your life. For you. And no matter what neckline you are wearing, practice good posture, wear it with a confident smile and you will carry it off beautifully.

Be willing to look a good long, validating look at yourself and acknowledge your body size, shape and skin tones. What is going to be right for you can only be determined by realizing what inimitable gifts you have to work with:

❖ What height are you? *If you are very tall, why not go with a lower heel. If shorter, perhaps a higher heel is best. Are you even comfortable in heels? If not, don't wear them. There are plenty of gorgeous shoes that will be comfortable for you.*

❖ Are you large breasted or small? *If you are self-conscious about small breasts, try a top with ruching. Or about large ones, you may want to stay away from fabric that clings.*

❖ Do you have narrow or broad shoulders? *Décolletage works beautifully on a wider chest.*

❖ Is your neck a bit long or shorter? *Either way a silk scarf can be gorgeous if draped properly.*

❖ Are you a hat person? *Add a few to your wardrobe.*

❖ Are your legs lean or thick? *Find a length in pants or skirts that feels most comfortable and works best for you. There are always flattering options.*

❖ Is your waist slim or large? *Will a belt be flattering? If so, select the right width one for you.*

❖ Do you have curves or straight lines? *If you are trying to look a bit slimmer, skin tight probably is not the best choice. Try a looser fit.*

You know better than anyone else what you want to achieve with your wardrobe. You have some gut level idea about what you want to say in your fashion statement, but you don't always trust your judgment. This may be because there are times you buy into societal pressures.

Don't do it. Don't get stuck thinking that what someone else is seeing in their mirror is more "right" than what you are seeing in yours. Don't buy into that trap. Honor the reflection in your looking glass and don't worry about anyone else's reflection in theirs.

Throughout the process of determining what you have to work and what you are trying to achieve, you may want to do some research. Reading this book is a good start. Later, you may want to go to a professional, just be sure it is one with more than just a motive to sell you something.

How about asking a girlfriend? Just make it one who can be objective, who will tell you the truth. There is nothing wrong with asking for help in this process. Actually, it's half the fun and you will likely find yourself helping them as much as they are helping you. Together you can weed out what's not great and what is. Be willing to try lots of different things in this process of elimination. Keep in mind that with every outfit, what looks good on someone else doesn't have to look good on you. And all the while, know that it isn't personal, but that you are simply gathering information.

Sometimes you may be tempted to get caught up in trends. Don't get caught in thinking that just because this season's latest fad is being touted as the only way to go, that it's the way for you. There are options for every fashion season and always have been, but often we don't notice because we aren't open-minded.

In the 1950s and early '60s, the style most remembered was hourglass waists on big belted dresses with wide skirts. I never wore them then, I didn't wear them when they came back in the '80s, and I wouldn't wear them now. I knew they weren't right for me, but were better on women with small waists and big hips. Because it wasn't my best look, I found my way around it. I never focused on what "they said" was in style and still don't. It just never upset me if something didn't suit me, because I was always excited about finding things that did. Working on movie projects, for every time period, I could always offer an actor something to wear other than the supposed "in" thing. I simply had to look.

As you age, accepting and respecting that you will change is important. See if you can adapt to these changes instead of fighting against them. Don't force something to work that doesn't. It's not only OK to acknowledge our age, our potentially lighter skin tones, gray hair or our wrinkles, but it is a beautiful part of the process.

Your willingness to accept who you are and where you are at in life will always shine through. That way, no matter what you are wearing, it will look better, guaranteed. Part of your wardrobe statement should be your confidence with who you are, at whatever stage of life you are in.

If you are a bit more "mature," you might not want to wear stark clothing colors against gray hair, simply because it may not look best. Any wrinkles you may have can appear magnified against the dark hues. Instead of seeing it as "*I can't wear this anymore because it looks terrible,*" why not think of it as "*I look great in that.*" Work at viewing yourself with a positive slant instead of a negative one. With understanding where *not* to go with fashion you can begin to develop a sense of where *to* go with it and let the real you shine through.

Taking my own advice, I recently hung my black turtlenecks up for good. Well, maybe not for good, but I don't wear them very much. They're just not my best choice anymore, now that I am a little older and of course wiser, which is certainly a nice byproduct. I suggest for you to be willing to do the same. To accept what does not work best for you and focus instead on what does.

Chapter Four
True Colors

Know your Color Story

∞ ∞ ∞ ∞

"The best color in the whole world
is the one that looks good on you."
Coco Chanel

Choosing what colors are the best for you is not an easy task and requires some work. Your skin color, the color of your eyes, your age – all of that is important. Blonds with very light skin often look better in soft colors. With darker skin and darker hair, bright intense colors typically work well. If you have blue or green eyes, something in shades of these colors next to your face will intensify the color of your eyes.

Sometimes, a stark black on a high collar is too much of a contrast. For me today, I feel like every wrinkle becomes more pronounced if I wear this look and I'd rather play them down with lighter colors. I'm OK with this realization and it doesn't mean I don't wear black. I still do all the time, but I prefer it with softer necklines and in pieces that are more flattering for me today.

So, how do you decide which colors work for you and which don't? How do you write your color story? What if it changes over time? What helps you determine what shades are your "must haves"? I'm sure you've heard the terms *warm* and *cool* as they relate to colors. To simplify, *cool* speaks to shades of green, blue and purple. *Warm* is largely made up of oranges, reds and yellows. But, these guidelines are not exactly "black and white."

Many women learn about what cool and warm means to them the hard way, with regard to their hair color. Most of you have heard either that you need "*an ash base to your shade,*" or that "*golden undertones are the way to go,*" right? You're not really sure what that means, until you and your best girlfriend decide to color your own hair. You select the exact same shade. Let's say "Blonde #27" just for fun and you get right to it. Putting your gloves on, you're ready to go.

The timer goes off and you are fully processed according to the directions and yet, after you both wash your hair and stand before the mirror, hers is gorgeous and yours looks nothing like "Blonde #27" and more like "Red #35." Same shade, same directions, same processing time, so how does this happen?

The answer is that we all have very different skin and hair undertones. It's important to learn what yours are. And perhaps even more importantly, when it comes to hair, from now on go to a really good salon for an expert to do what they do best. Allow yourself to be pampered, especially since one of the greatest wardrobe assets you can have is a beautiful hairstyle that suits you in both shade and form. You don't want to skimp in this area.

I have personal experience in the hair arena and know how difficult it can be to find and maintain a shade. Back in the 1990s, my hair color was light brown with red highlights. Once, I was on location in Luxemburg and planning a vacation in Europe right after the filming I was involved in. Because I wanted to have my hair done before I left, I asked my assistant to make an appointment for me with a hairdresser she had suggested.

The only appointment available was during my lunch break. Unfortunately, my assistant couldn't join me, so I had to go by myself. As it turns out, the hairdresser didn't speak English and I couldn't speak German or French, so our communication was limited at best. After numerous "*Oui, Madam's*" it became obvious that from a light brunette, I had turned into a blond! It was quite a shock for everyone when I came back to the set when I returned a few hours later. Luckily, as it turns out, I loved the new color and not only did I sport it during my European travels, I maintained it with a colorist back home.

But, sometime later, I had to go to Europe for work on the film *The Peacemaker* with George Clooney and Nicole Kidman. Before I left, I asked my colorist to give me her formula to keep up my new hair color while I was on location. While there, our hairdresser on the set applied the formula and much to my horror, my hair turned green! I remember George Clooney jokingly consoling me, *"At least now your hair matches the color of my military uniform."* I can chuckle now, but the moral of the story is to use a good specialist.

If you indeed decide to radically change the color of your hair, my suggestion is to first go to a wig store and try various colors and styles. That way you won't regret your decision. After all, that's what we always did when trying to create a new character on the film sets.

Whether you are looking to change your color or just get a cut, I can suggest a website that may help you find a terrific salon no matter what city in the world you are in:

http://www.leadingsalons.com

So, now that you have a brief idea of undertone, you may want to go deeper, to determine how it relates to your own color story. First, what are your general characteristics? Are you *light* or *dark*? It may be very easy to tell. Think of sultry Salma Hayek versus light and airy Goldie Hawn. If you are dark, your eyes are likely to be deep brown, dark green or even black and your hair is may be bold shades of brown or black. If light, your eyes will tend more towards pale green, blue, or even a gentle gold and your hair is usually blonde or a light shade of brown.

But what if your coloring isn't that cut and dry? What if your characteristics fall more in between the two? That's where cool and warm tones come into play. What describes you best? Are you warm with medium shades in your hair (golden brown, copper, auburn) and eyes that are brown or dark green? Or are you cool with hair that is ash toned (gray, silver) and eyes that are violet, charcoal gray or a soft shade of blue?

You will want to determine what your skin tone is. This can vary on a scale from *warm* to *cool.* I encourage you to visit websites that will help you to determine yours so that you can be guided towards colors that will work fabulously for you. Here are a few:

Thechicfashionista.com

Cardiganempire.com

Truth-is-beauty.com

Let's say you've determined your color palette. Now you want your wardrobe to reflect the best options for you, but you're unsure how to go about it. A color analyst can be extremely helpful in assisting you by working with color swatches. They will often drape various ones over you in an effort to determine what works best for you within a color family.

Let's admit it - on some level you know what's right for you. You know what you like when it comes to color and what you don't. As for me, I never wore pink in my life. I didn't feel I looked good in it, so even if it's the "color of the season" I am still not going to wear pink. You probably know many of the shades that work for you already, as well as the ones that don't. Usually a person's closet reflects colors that someone is drawn to.

Let's say you decide you need a change, so you take your hair several shades lighter or darker. Remember, if you do, your wardrobe may have to be updated a bit. What worked for you before may not be your best option now.

When your hair color changes, either by choice or by nature, you want to be willing to make some color changes in your closet. If you are sporting more of a tan, this will also open up different choices. What color looks good with your hair shade and skin tone now? Are they a bit lighter or darker than they used to be? If so, adjust your wardrobe and makeup accordingly. But, sometimes you may decide that something simply isn't for you. In my case, if I didn't wear pink 10 years ago, why would I think it'll look good this season just because it's "the favorite color?"

I remember working on a film once when lime green was "the hot trend." The leading actress came to me insisting, "*I want to wear lots of lime green for this movie because it's so in this season.*" I remember asking her, "*Do you want people to appreciate this movie in ten years or just for this season?*" The look on her face told me it had registered. "*By the way,*" I continued, "*we haven't even determined whether that color will look good on you. I don't imagine that you want future movie going generations to say, 'What was she thinking?'*"

Color choice matters in fashion. It can often make a statement. Have you ever noticed that certain colors affect your mood or how you feel towards others? There may be times to consider what you wear carefully because it can determine how others see you as well as how you "see" yourself that day while you wear it. An example is a fashion choice for a job interview. Conservative colors will usually be best for a first impression. Navy, tan and gray are often good options, especially in the corporate arena. You usually can't go wrong with one of these.

What about color in general? Think of the color *red*. When you wear it, are you a bit more feisty and energetic? Do you feel more alive? When you see someone wearing this color, do they grab your attention? There has been a great deal of research on Color Psychology and how certain colors represent specific ideas and impressions to us:

Red – attract attention, bold, the color of the "power" tie you see at election time; aggressive; assertive; energy and strength; definitely no shrinking violet.

Blue - success, loyalty, authority; the color of the ocean, the sky; the navy blue power suit; Greeks used this color to ward off the evil eye.

Gray – serious; business-like; efficient.

Silver – strong; helpful; wise.

Brown – down to earth; security; reliable.

Beige/Tan – approachable; slightly informal; warm; friendly.

Black – a little more complicated. 1. The elegance of a black tie event, chic, casual success; the little black flirty dress. But sometimes: 2. somber, funereal; inconspicuous.

Gold – success; personal power; glitz; glamour; style; confidence.

Yellow – playful; casual; cheerful; good times.

Pink – confident; daring.

Purple – majestic; mysterious; regal.

White – pure; clean; crisp; fresh.

Green – color of money; nature; conservative, good luck.

These color "meanings" are generalizations. If you find shades that work for you, by all means wear them and don't worry about what they might represent! But be sure that whatever you wear, you are wearing it on your terms.

Just a few quick words about makeup – my rule is *"Less is More."* I have learned that with age, heavy makeup and too dark colors can sometimes make you look older. By day you may want to avoid heavy shadows or dark pencil around your eyes. Darker makeup colors often look better at night and it may be best to use creamy shadows over powdered ones. Be careful with lip colors and find a neutral lip liner to fill in your whole lip before applying lipstick. This will help with any feathering or lipstick "bleeding."

What color do you feel like *being* today? Keep in mind that sometimes, even after all the determinations you make of warm vs. cool or light vs. dark, it will simply come down to that and you can keep it really simple. Be clear that you believe in yourself and in your choice and that will make all the difference.

Chapter Five
Properly Dressed for Every Occasion

What to Wear Where

∞ ∞ ∞ ∞ ∞

"A girl should be two things: classy and fabulous."
Coco Chanel

How do you decide what to wear when you are going out? Do you find yourself frustrated when getting ready, unsure whether the event you are going to warrants dressing down or dressing up? Have you ever worn something that made you uncomfortable once you arrived at the party and you wished that you'd opted for something else? Have you felt a little less socially comfortable than you would have liked because of what you had on? Have you ever missed the mark with your fashion choice?

How do you know what to wear for a casual event, making sure that it isn't too casual? When is dressy too dressy? These questions come up all the time.

Society seems to have gotten more laid back in general. It's often acceptable to be "dressed down," but do you sometimes take it too literally? Do you wonder how some people can wear a tee shirt and jeans and look like a million bucks when you feel sloppy in the same outfit? Loafers, jeans and a crisp white tee can be great "go-to's" as long as the clothes are pressed and fresh. Keep in mind that a light touch with an iron can go a long way in making the difference between tousled and pristine. The best part about these staple items is that if you throw a fabulous blazer over them, you can be dressed up in a flash.

You may have heard the expression, "You are not so rich as to have cheap clothes." It is one I grew up with and I think it says a lot. When opting for casual style, it's important not to mistake what that means. Casual does not mean cheap. It doesn't mean inexpensive, although it may if you get a fabulous bargain. Casual style is not meant to be messy. Instead, it is smart, comfortable and simple. Often, when we see someone dressed casually, it seems to have happened by accident. But, it is very probably no accident.

It all starts with what you have hanging in your closet or folded in your drawers. How many times have you bought something trendy because you simply *had* to have it? You loved the idea of it and purchased it without paying much attention to the quality, because it was a "must have" in all the magazines. The problem though, was that you only got to wear it a few times before having to replace it. It didn't hold up that well, keep its shape or color and you never felt quite comfortable wearing it because it didn't really fit right.

On the other hand, whenever you have gone with classic style, it seemed to last forever. Wearing it, you find yourself feeling not only comfortable, but confident. The fantastic white linen blouse that cost a fortune when you paid for it has come in handy for ages. The jeans that were almost the price of a car payment have never gone out of style. The perfect light weight sweaters or jacket that you've worn with everything are like trusted friends. The loafers that were way over your budget when you got them turn out to be a steal in the long run. This is casual style.

It is much better to have just a few pieces that are quality than many items that aren't. Part of smart style means knowing how to have staples in your wardrobe that you can wear with anything. Ones that will last. Things you can wear over and over in different ways that will hold up well.

Keep in mind that a more expensive price tag doesn't guarantee fabulous. It may not be your right fit. The cut of some designer's clothing just doesn't work for me. Look for things that fit well and have staying power when building the casual section of your wardrobe, as well as the dressier side. Be willing to pay for what you get. Remember, *"You are not so rich as to have cheap clothes."*

Of course not everyone can afford expensive prices. But don't be fooled into thinking you are getting a better deal when buying several low priced items instead of just one for the same dollar amount. Buy quality and you can't go wrong, whether you are buying it to dress up or dress down. I really believe it is better to not buy anything at all than to buy something *cheap*. In my own line this concept is very important, which is why our clothing is very high quality yet still affordable.

Let's face it, if you are young and in great shape, you can get away with trendy pieces that are less structurally sound. Even if something is baggy on you or doesn't fit that well, you can probably pull it off. But if you are a little bit older, opt for a piece or two that have to keep their shape. A structured jacket is a good choice, because it won't hang awkwardly. And remember, if something looks cheap, it's cheap. There's no way around it.

If you can afford to change your wardrobe every season, by all means do so. Go all out! If not, spend money on the basics. Pick things like high quality blouses and slacks, great shoes, structured jackets and well-made leggings that will all hold up. Yes, trends change, but a good jacket or dress that has staying power will work for you through many seasons. And again, if you are watching your budget, be careful. Instead of buying five or six shirts that will soon fade and lose their shape, buy one or two that are better quality and can be worn with everything. Just accessorize them differently.

One accessory that works fabulously in many arenas is the scarf. I own them in every color and width and encourage you to do the same. A great scarf can be used to update or add a twist to a basic outfit. Go to my website: www.komarovinc.com for a short tutorial on how to wear our textured scarves in many different ways. Whether you are looking to appear casual, chic or elegant, you can tout the same scarf. It can be worn in various ways to work, lunch or a cocktail party. Depending on the effect you want to achieve, you can add a gorgeous brooch, drape your shoulders or simply add color to your blouse's neckline.

When you are going to the gym or exercising, casual style can be a little different. This is when I often wear a trendy tee shirt. I sometimes buy one even though I know it may only last through a few washings. I know it's likely to shrink or nap, but am OK with it because it's fun to get new ones and it is not too expensive. But with leggings, I never opt for inexpensive. You have to get ones that will keep their shape and hold up well.

Laid back society or not, there are still times and places where casual just won't do. Major life events such as a wedding, a Bar Mitzvah or opening nights are occasions to go all out. Sometimes you are expected to dress up and other times you just feel like it. It's important to have items in your closet that make it easy to do so no matter what the reason.

Dressing for Interviews:

An important time to focus on what you wear is when you have a job interview. Remember, first impressions go a long way. Often an interviewer makes a decision whether or not to call someone back in the first few seconds. Be conscious of what you wear and how you appear in it. You will want to dress appropriately in the right type of clothing for a work environment. Try to stay away from flashy patterns or too loud colors. Gray and navy are excellent choices. Be sure your apparel fits well and isn't either too baggy or too tight.

If you want to appear well groomed, be sure your clothing doesn't look wrinkled. If it does, it can seem as if you didn't take the interview seriously enough to prepare for it. It may cause doubts about how much attention you would put into work if you were hired. Set the right tone for your interview by looking professional.

Your Wardrobe and Commuting:

If you commute for business, you want to wear something that will look as fresh when you arrive at work as it did when you put it on. This isn't always easy, so you have to be sure to select the right fabrics – the ones that don't wrinkle and that have staying power like the pleated garments we offer at Komarov Inc.

Many young women spend a great deal of time commuting to work. If you are one of them, you probably fall into one of two scenarios:

❖ You work in a downtown area but live in the suburbs. Let's say Los Angeles and the Valley. Your rush hour commute takes an hour or so, therefore going home to change before a night out is simply not worth it. The good news is that since you drive, you can toss a garment bag in the car for the quick change at the end of the day. After work, put on a fabulous chiffon tiered dress and your latest shoes from Christian Louboutin.

❖ You take a commuter rail, perhaps from Grand Central Station to Connecticut each day, so you don't have a trunk to work with. You really can't tote a whole new outfit in your briefcase and don't feel like carting one around anyway, so you opt for a good pair of pants and a nice jacket for the day. After work you can lose the jacket and be date ready. Or simply bring a pair of higher heels, together with some jewelry, along for the evening. Carrying one item is doable, where a whole outfit may not be.

Either way, you have to plan out what you wear. This is why I suggest that many of your clothes be selections that can be dressed up or dressed down. You don't want to go out feeling like you are still in work mode at night do you? It's a bit easier now that many workplaces are not as formal as they used to be, but if yours is not office casual, give yourself plenty of simple adjustment options for your outfit once your day is done.

There will be some occasions where you absolutely want to go home and freshen up "après work." You may simply want a shower and a new face of makeup. But if not, select wardrobe choices that allow you to move between different arenas effortlessly.

Workday Attire:

If you spend your days in corporate America or in court, you may require a suit. If so, be sure it is well

64

tailored. You want to make certain that it's not either hanging on you or too snug, but fits well and looks sharp. In a conservative environment, neutral colors are a good choice. If you have a little flexibility and can get away with it, use accessories to add a little flair. When meeting a new client, find out a bit about them before you make a wardrobe blunder. If they are staid and old fashioned, keep it conservative. If fun and artistic, it may be OK to be more colorful with your clothing choice for that meeting.

Let's say you decide to wear a dress to the office, be sure that it's not too clingy or revealing. Be conscious of your shoes. Super high, spike heels are not usually a good choice for the average work place. If your office is casual, by all means dress that way. But keep in mind that you are at work and be professional and neat in whatever you decide to wear.

Home Office Wardrobe:

When working from home, comfort is key and of course casual is fine. But just because you are not dressing for the office, you still will benefit from dressing for yourself. It can help to set an organized, neat mood for your day. Staying in pajama bottoms and a tee shirt may not be the best way to do that. Good leggings with a long tunic or a comfy knit dress are better choices for your home office. When you need a break, simply put on a pair of sandals and you are ready to head out. Don't let yourself be sloppy just because you work from home. You'll find yourself more productive if you take a little time on your apparel, even when you don't have to leave the house.

When you dress, pay attention to detail. Snip off loose threads and check for missing buttons. That will reflect on how you come across, not just in business situations but all the time. Be conscious of first impressions no matter where you are making them. Always check your shoes for scuff marks and buff them if necessary so that you look crisp and neat. It's amazing what a difference worn out or dull shoes can make to an outfit. Always be sure yours are in good shape. Think enough of yourself to be prepared. It will go a long way in others seeing you that way.

Special Occasions:

For special occasions, dress up. Period. That is my advice. Accepting certain invitations creates a reason for going all out. That's half the fun of saying yes to them. My collection is filled with dresses that are versatile, but the section for "special occasion dresses" is just that, special. Sometimes you need really extraordinary choices, ultra feminine ones that make you feel prettier in them. Be sure to have a few pairs of shoes to wear with them. Shoes that are perhaps higher heeled, more frilly or just plain fun to wear. Ones that give you that lift you need to help you exude confidence and femininity.

Mother of the Bride or Groom:

Some occasions are even more special than others. One example would be when you are the mother of a bride or groom. If you are in this role, you will of course want to look fabulous. As much as this day is an important one for your son or daughter, it is for you as well. You should look elegant, but not upstage the bride. Selecting your dress can be very challenging.

As a mother of the groom myself, I remember searching up and down Rodeo Drive for the right dress to wear to my son's wedding. I felt almost as excited about what to wear for this event as I had for my own wedding many years before. After searching and not finding anything I loved, I made the dress myself. Because of my own experience, *Komarov Inc.* specializes in dresses for this category.

Along this vein, we know that weddings typically have a color story. This is why we offer dresses that will tie in handsomely as part of any color theme. We also have jackets and shawls in our collections to coordinate with any piece you may choose. Often, women prefer to cover their arms as they get a little bit older and if this is the case for you, we want to make sure you have everything you need for a very special day.

Après Work:

If, after work, you have a dinner date you'll want to wear something smashing that day, but you may not be able to get away with it at the office. Why not don a skirt with opaque stockings and a conservative blouse from nine to five and later switch to sheers and open a few buttons. You can always add a great necklace and a few bracelets and be date ready in a flash.

If you are married or in a committed relationship, note what your partner will be wearing when you are going out. Is he or she wearing a jacket or suit or are they going casual? Part of good taste is being in sync and looking appropriate in any situation.

Keep in mind that the way you are likely to wear a dress to work will be different from the way you will wear it to dinner or dancing afterwards. Drape a scarf over your neckline for day and remove it at night or tie it differently later to create a more feminine effect. Wear a jacket over a dress to work and consider "losing" the jacket later. With a versatile dress, you may only have to change your shoes and add a few jewelry accessories to go from day to night.

Dressing up a conservative outfit is fun and it's really not that hard to do. I personally believe in having a closet full of clothes that you can dress up or dress down. It was a huge part of my planning process when designing my clothing line. Looking great, being comfortable and having versatile choices all came into play, and in fact still do as we add pieces. Your wardrobe should be filled with clothing that you can take from a meeting to a social event easily.

This is a key factor in choosing pieces for my own wardrobe, especially when I travel.

Look over your wardrobe periodically. Check each piece carefully and don't put anything back in the closet unless it's in clean, crisp, and ready to wear shape. This will help on those days when you are rushed in getting ready. You don't want to realize too late that something was hanging that actually had to go to the dry cleaner. Don't be caught off guard. A little simple planning in advance will save time in dressing, no matter what you are getting ready for.

Suppose you will be going out with the girls for dinner after five. In that case you can go a bit more casual because you don't have to impress your friends. Maybe you can just add a fun beaded sweater right over your work dress. A different pair of shoes may do the trick, something with a higher heel perhaps. Or if you are wearing a skirt to the office, tote a pair of great jeans to change into later. But either way, if you have to be at your desk all day and won't have time to go home to change, you will want to think through your morning wardrobe selection carefully and plan accordingly.

I love spending time with friends and do so often. Whether it's a quick lunch or a full afternoon, I enjoy relaxing with them or sometimes bouncing work ideas off those I am close to. Because my schedule is busy, friends and business often overlap. I regularly have to juggle work and social events and have to "change hats" several times a day. I may have a fashion show, luncheon, several business meetings and a dinner obligation all in one day. If so, I'll have to be dressed in a way that would be appropriate for all of it. I have to plan accordingly so that I can feel as coiffed at dinner as I do at breakfast and lunch, even though I won't have time to change in between.

I hate when my clothes are wrinkled late in the day, so I strive to maintain a fresh look. To give you some idea of how particular I am in that, I still like my sheets freshly ironed. Of course I chuckle at myself because nobody does that anymore, but that speaks to how freshly pressed I like to feel. It reminds me of a story that was influential in my clothing line being launched.

I've traveled around the world over the years, but one trip really stands out. I was on a trip with a friend one spring. After finishing a shoot for the miniseries *Sinatra* in Hoboken, New Jersey, my friend the production designer on *Sinatra* and I decided to stay in New York for a few days. It was springtime and we wanted to enjoy the lovely weather, with *The Plaza Hotel* as our base. One evening, after having been out and about, we returned to our room to freshen up before going to the landmark *Russian Tea Room*. It had been a fabulous day with perfect weather and we both had worn linen outfits. The clothes were terribly wrinkled, typical for linen after a few hours, and we wanted to press them before going for dinner.

Of course guests at *The Plaza* are not accustomed to ironing their own clothing, so when we contacted the concierge, we were told they didn't have an iron available. We could, however, have our items dry cleaned and returned to our room within twenty four hours. Well, since we wanted to wear them that night, this wouldn't work.

We tried steaming the wrinkles out in the bathroom to no avail. So, we wound up stepping out to *The Russian Tea Room* on West 57th Street feeling like two unmade beds. We were terribly uncomfortable at first, but wound up relaxing over our blinis with caviar. Chuckling, my friend asked, "How do real people live and take care of their clothing without a trailer and ten assistants? What do they do without wardrobe departments to iron or steam their clothes? It seems impossible." I remember her insisting, "*Shelley, you have to figure something out. You should create some beautiful clothes that will be easy to travel with. It will be perfect because everyone wants great things that are easy to take care of. Everyone will want them.*"

This conversation was what led to our coming up with the fabulous pleating system we use for our dresses. It was how the concept for the company was born. It still makes me laugh when I think of going out in those linen suits.

Chapter Six
Traveling Light

∞ ∞ ∞ ∞

"If you wish to travel far and fast, travel light. Take off your envies, jealousies, unforgiveness, selfishness and fears."
Cesare Pavese

When we traveled for movie projects, every single outfit was packed in tissue and ironed to perfection. We even had special dry cleaners who went above and beyond, returning clothes in record time. I remember being in Slovakia on location and having our hotel hand wash whatever we needed. The average person who travels today is not going to have exposure to this type of care for their clothing.

People travel all the time now for both work and pleasure. It may be for long weekend getaways, sightseeing trips throughout the United States or overseas, much needed vacations away from work, family visits or short business trips. Whatever the reason for the trip, focus carefully on what you pack. You will want to be prepared for wherever you are traveling to and for whatever may come up while you are there.

The first thing to consider is whether or not you are going for business or pleasure, so that your suitcase will be properly filled. Will there be meetings or parties to attend? Do you need formal wear or are you strictly going to relax? What type of items do you obviously need? Which ones do you want on hand just in case? It's always best to bring a bit of everything just to have your bases covered.

But, since airlines charge for extra bags nowadays, how can you do that without spending a fortune? To avoid paying for extras, you don't want to over-pack with something you never use later. Consider key pieces. Select items that can be worn in several different ways and color coordinate. Mix and match. Intertwine some pieces into more than one outfit.

It's hard, when you are standing looking into a suitcase at home, to think about everything you will need once you get to where you are going. First of all, you have to think about what the weather is like there. You want to be prepared whatever the weather. Versatile items are key.

How about accessories? Having to cart too many of these can be a nuisance, so why not base your trip's wardrobe around a specific color scheme? That way you can pack lightly, have whatever accessories you need and be sure everything works together. Clothes that can be used for different outfits are ideal when traveling.

Once you narrow down the basics, figure out what pieces you have within that color scheme that will work well in different scenarios. Keep things as low maintenance as possible. What you pack should be comfortable, easy to wear and shouldn't wrinkle easily. Who wants to press clothes when they are on vacation? And even if you are willing, there may not be an iron available to you depending on where you stay. Take it from me.

The right shoes are important. You will want to make sure they are versatile. First, they take up a lot of room in a suitcase so you won't want to pack a different pair for each outfit. Second, make sure they are stylish but comfortable. You don't want to be sightseeing with sore feet, but you also want to look fashionable. Keep in mind that you may not be able to find a replacement pair while traveling. Once, a friend was visiting Japan and found a pair of shoes she liked. When she asked the clerk for her size, eight, she was told, "*We don't carry men's sizes.*" And always be sure to throw in an extra pair of stockings just to be prepared.

Carefully consider what you pack in your carry-on luggage, because it can be a complete disaster if your luggage is lost. Pack smart so that you know that whatever you carry on could possibly be worn on the whole trip in an emergency.

I've had travel disasters myself when luggage has gotten lost. Once I went from Scottsdale, Arizona, where I'd attended a meeting with *Nordstrom* and *Dillard's*, to New York for a three day fashion Coterie and my luggage was lost. My schedule from the moment I arrived was back to back meetings and my calendar was completely full. Therefore, I had absolutely no time to shop for replacement clothes.

For the entire three days I was dressed in the black pants that I'd worn on the plane and my husband's tee shirts. The only thing I could change were the tee shirts, because they were readily available to me. "Only" ten days later, and certainly not very timely, my luggage was returned to me back in Los Angeles.

Any time I travel now, this experience rests in the back of my mind. I always wear something versatile, stylish and comfortable on the plane just in case. I also consider very carefully what is in my carry-on bag so, to the best of my ability, I avoid any misplaced luggage disasters.

Don't pack lots of extra clothes that you never use. Bring items that you can wear more than once. Be willing to mix things up unless, of course, you are traveling for a specific function like a wedding or black tie, where special pieces and accessories will likely be required. In that case, of course bring whatever is needed and don't skimp because you'll want to look amazing. You may want to consider putting any items for your special event in a garment bag and carrying them on the plane just to be on the safe side though.

I remember a situation a friend encountered when he traveled from Los Angeles to Korea for a few days some years back. His luggage was lost, so when he arrived in Korea he had nothing to change into. Unfortunately the only clothes he had were the ones he'd worn on the plane, which were jeans and a tee shirt. The next morning he had to be in a very important meeting at a corporation there, but his attire was absolutely inappropriate.

He asked his hotel concierge where he could buy some emergency clothes and was led to a few places. The problem was that he was a size Extra Large, which was not the norm by any means in Korea. Men are typically smaller there, so he couldn't find anything to fit. He had to settle on the largest shirt he could find which was not large enough for him. He got away with it, but the sleeves came only ¾ of the way down his arms and ended at the elbow. He'd had no other choice.

When I think of this story, it reminds me of how important it is to be prepared and I always wear something on the plane that is versatile, just in case. Always be ready for surprises.

Lastly, I always like to leave just a little bit of room in my bag for a souvenir piece or two from my travels. I often find something really special and don't like to feel stressed about how I will lug it home. There are often unique and different clothing items available in other parts of the world and I like to be able to take them away with me as reminders of a great trip.

Chapter Seven
Trends

∞ ∞ ∞ ∞

"Don't be into trends. Don't make fashion own you,

but you decide who you are, what you want to express

by the way you dress and the way you live."

Gianni Versace

I'd like to address the history of fashion and what "to be fashionable" or "to be on trend" means. Throughout time, people have tried to push the envelope by setting new trends. But in conjunction with that, limits of what is acceptable have been put in place.

A few curious examples as they relate to shoe trends:

❖ Sandals with marked soles. That's what prostitutes in ancient Greece wore to leave seductive messages to their clients.

❖ Platform shoes, although seemingly a trend of "our time," were worn in the Middle Ages.

❖ A 17th century law stipulated a limit on the height of a shoe's heel to prevent pregnant women from falling and causing harm to their unborn babies.

❖ The Massachusetts Puritan Colony banned woman from wearing heels, because they were deemed to be a tool of seduction.

❖ In France, Louis XIV imposed a strict rule that only he and his court were allowed to wear shoes with red soles. Luckily, times change and if you can afford a pair of Louboutin's, you too can wear red soles!

When you think of extravagant fashion, your thoughts may be limited to women, but this arena is not just a female domain. Examples go back many centuries of men taking fashion risks. In the middle of the 18th century there was a trend known as *macaroni*. It was set by a group of young, wealthy Englishmen who took a Grand Tour through Italy and shocked the society by their outlandish costumes.

Their name was derived from the pasta of the same name, which they surely enjoyed during their travels in the country. Just an aside, but the line in the song *Yankee Doodle* speaks to this group of men – "*stuck a feather in his cap and called it macaroni.*"

These men adopted the flamboyant continental styles of France and Italy but took every detail to extremes. Towering elaborate wigs were worn with tiny hats perched atop them. They sported garishly patterned waistcoats which clashed with their brightly colored stockings. So, step aside, Lady Gaga and Madonna, the world has seen, time and again, many examples of men's fashion as it startles and shocks.

Fashion as a business started under Colbert, French Minister of Finance under Louis XIV. He instituted many economic reforms in an attempt to improve the French economy and was responsible for bringing many artisans from all over Europe to France. These included Venetian mirror makers from Murano who established production of mirrors in France, with the French court becoming the first customers. Very soon the French court became the most fashionable trend setter in Europe. Incidentally, during the French Revolution it was the Russian court, which admired everything French, that saved the French manufacturers from total collapse.

For centuries, changes in fashion were relatively slow. With rapid industrialization, especially during the twentieth century, the fashion industry experienced dramatic changes. Now a huge industry, it's pieces and parts must consistently change and grow in order to compete. Launching new trends is one of the ways to make changes. So, now every season we look to be on trend, whether it is in colors, in shapes or in lengths.

One costume designer's rule as it comes to changing trends is that if you don't want your selected wardrobe to appear dated on screen, keep "fad" pieces out of it. This is actually a pretty safe idea. If you look at some classic movies made in the 1940s, you will see that shoulder pads were often used in the wardrobes even before their time. This may be because some in Hollywood didn't think as much about what was correct for the period the film was based in as they did about how something would look on an actress. The star could often dictate what they wanted and that's what was used even if it wasn't exactly correct for an era.

Watching a film and seeing shoulder pads in period films before their time is a bit awkward when you are a stickler for detail the way I am. I worked hard to be authentic with my costumes, just as I do with my personal wardrobe. Don't be afraid to be authentic yourself. Sure, it's nice to follow trends, but be careful. You don't want your clothes to look dated when you wear them after the fad is over. And bottom line, if a trend doesn't work for you don't go with it. If everyone is wearing a color this season that isn't your best one, don't wear it. Don't be a slave to fashion trends with either your casual style or your "dressed up" one. Fashion can be very cruel to you or it can be your dear friend. Strive for the latter.

Just recently I found myself in the valet parking line after a big pre-Oscar Costume Designers Guild annual party at the *Beverly Hilton Hotel* in Beverly Hills. A few of our costume designers were waiting in line holding their shoes (fabulous designer ones such as Louboutin) in their hands. One standing next to me, who was just nominated for Oscar, muttered, "*Yes, they look good, but to wear them!*" Well, maybe she was unfamiliar with a quote from Christian Louboutin himself: "*I would hate for someone to look at my shoes and say, Oh my God! They look so comfortable.*" Lately, I prefer shoes that I can wear all night!

When you see the latest style trend, it's not necessary to get upset knowing it simply won't work for you. That doesn't have to be a bad thing. In fact, it may mean that when you go out for one of the year's most important evenings, you won't be dressed similar to anyone else.

One of the things I love about Paris is that you don't see obvious trends that much. I am there twice a year and what I see are people looking elegant. If ruffles are a trend, it doesn't mean that the whole country is wearing them. Actually, I personally don't like ruffles, so whether they are in or out, in Paris or the United States, I won't be wearing them. It's so much more fun to work trends into your own style than to be dictated to by what you see in magazines. Use these publications yes, just as I did back at *Hermitage* when I pored over the library of them there, but just for ideas, not to give you absolute rules.

That's not to say you don't want to pay attention to the latest fashion ideas, because of course you do. But, make trends work for you, not the other way around. Don't be affected by what you are told you should be wearing. When you are standing holding your chardonnay at the season's biggest cocktail party, you want to be noticed as original you, not as the outfit you might have been expected to wear because "it's in."

I don't want to be dressed exactly the same as anyone else when I am at a function, but I insist on being stylish. That may mean something slightly different depending on where I am going. What should be worn to a small cocktail party at a friends' house is very different than at a Hollywood one. But at whichever party I attend, the trick is to maintain individual style and elegance while looking smashing.

Chapter Eight
Lessons from Hollywood Experience

∞ ∞ ∞ ∞ ∞

"Everyone's a star and deserves the right to twinkle."

Marilyn Monroe

Adding a lighter touch to this book, I would like to share a few episodes from my career in Hollywood, choosing those that are relevant to the book's subject and often quite amusing, Since this is a book on style, I can't think of anything more fitting than to start with my collaboration with the queen of style, the great Loretta Young.

I worked with Loretta Young in the 1980s on a couple of films. Her first movie after a 20 year absence from the screen was *Christmas Eve*, a film for NBC. Loretta was a major Hollywood star who won an Oscar for "The Farmer's Daughter" in 1947. However, she is probably remembered the most for her television show "The Loretta Young Show" (1953-1961).

Every week, in each episode, she opened the door in a new gown. All the famous designers at the time competed for a chance to create the gowns she would wear on those entrances. With every new episode the audience eagerly waited for a surprise within a spectacular entrance. And every new entrance was spectacular indeed!

I was fitting Loretta at one point and my producer asked me whether I would mind if Jean Louis, a famous Hollywood legend, was present at our fittings. I remember being surprised that he was still alive because he had been a legend for more than forty years and had worked with all the major movie stars including Rita Hayworth, Deborah Kerr, Judy Garland, Joan Crawford, Kim Novak, Marlene Dietrich, Shirley MacLaine, Marilyn Monroe and Loretta Young.

Anyway, Jean Louis, who was in his eighties when I met him, was a very close friend of Loretta and he'd designed many of her gowns. They actually married in 1993. During our fittings, which often took hours, he would come to her house and join us. Her housekeeper served us lunch and I was blessed to be able to listen to old Hollywood stories. It was really an incredible experience and certainly a window to the old Hollywood gossips.

At one of those fittings, Jean Louis told me about his first meeting with Marilyn Monroe. He had come to her house in Santa Monica and was met by her house keeper, because Marilyn was on the phone. Finally, forty minutes later Ms. Monroe came to meet him wearing nothing more than a fur coat over her naked body. Seeing his expression of surprise, she said *"You are a designer, so you have to see me."* His response was, *"Well, in this movie we'll have a lot of hats!"* He also told me that the famous dress that Marilyn Monroe wore when she sang *Happy Birthday Mr. President* was so tight that he'd actually had to sew it while she was wearing it. I considered it true fate when ten years later I had an opportunity to reproduce this dress in the miniseries *A Woman Named Jackie.*

Those fittings with Loretta were so precise that they built a strong foundation for my future work. This was at a time before the later trend of product placements, where companies offered their products directly to productions. Loretta appreciated the workmanship and took great care of our handmade clothes. She was well aware of what looked good on her and knew how to make an entrance. I remember that she liked to wear nude colored shoes because when she did so they made her legs look longer. I greatly admired her for not only her grace and posture, which made clothes look good right away, but also because she knew what was and wasn't important.

After we finished our first film, for which she received a Golden Globe, we had a lot of press events. For one of those events I was helping her get ready at her home while a limousine was already waiting for her outside. She rushed to the door in one of her famous hats (she loved hats and had a vast collection of them) when I noticed a huge run in her stocking. I asked her to change it but she looked at me and said, *"Don't worry, nobody's perfect."* That stuck with me.

In the old studio system a star came to the wardrobe department, where the designer would take measurements. Then, they would build the dress form according to those measurements, which eliminated a lot of fittings when building the costumes. I used the same method when I designed a gown for the stars. Because of this, some old timers never knew their real size. Today, since much of movie's wardrobe is bought, they don't go through the same process as years ago, but I remember one experience.

Sometime in the 1990s, I received a call from the Vice President of MGM, with whom I had worked before, with an offer to work on a film. It was a remake of the classic film from the 1950s "*Inherit the Wind*," based on the famous 1920s Monkey Trial. I accepted without even knowing who would be cast in this film. The pre-production period was going to be very short, so I had to start as soon as possible. I soon found out, to my excitement, that the two leading parts were being played by George C. Scott and Jack Lemmon.

A few days before the shooting started, Piper Laurie was also brought onto the film. I remembered Piper, a very slender, pretty, red haired woman, from her earlier years. To prepare her wardrobe for the fitting, I called to ask her size. "*I don't know my size,*" she replied. When I asked for an approximation she said, "*Ten or twelve, I guess, but I don't really know.*"

That posed a potential problem for me as sizes of the period costumes didn't correspond to the contemporary sizes since people actually were getting bigger every year. Of course, when I met Piper, I could see that the problem was more than just a potential one, because she was not at all a size ten or twelve. Preparing for the shooting was quite a challenge, but we became friends and she loved the *Komarov* clothes.

So, we have to know our size, to have a sense of our measurements, especially if we want to buy clothes in other countries. Let's say you are size *Small* in United States sizes. This does not necessarily mean that you will be *Small* on a European scale. A U.S. *Small* can be 44 or 46 in European sizes, which is more like *Medium* here. This same size would be *Large* in Asia. To complicate things more, different manufacturers use different standards. Our fit U.S. model with a perfect size *Small* would have been considered *Medium* twenty years ago. People are getting bigger! So, if you are not well familiar with a manufacturer, it will be best to try a piece before buying.

One of my memorable experiences with sizes happened during my work on *Kennedys of Massachusetts*. I had to prepare a scene set in 1939 with Joe Kennedy as the Ambassador to Great Britain. He was being received at Buckingham Palace and for that scene, I also had to dress the Royal Guards. I called Tim Angeles, the owner of the oldest costume rental house in England and asked for uniforms for the guards. He said that he had some from the period but they were very small. The biggest one was size 38. By today's standards, size 38 is Small. I had to ask the casting director to cast teenagers for the royal guards in order to make it work!

As we age, some parts of our bodies grow and some shrink, so that we may become one size on the top and another one on the bottom. I recommend finding a manufacturer that fits your specific needs. At *Komarov*, we address these issues, sometimes choosing different sizes for the tops and bottoms, which is very important for a dress. And, no matter what, make sure to have a correct undergarment, it can very helpfully change the fit.

Shelley on locations with:

1 Mathew McConahey (*Newton Boys*); 2 Halle Berry (*Introducing Dorothy Dandridge*); 3 George Clooney (*The Peacemaker*) ; 4 Jack Lemmon (*Inherit the Wind*); 5 Loretta Young (*Christmas Eve*)

1 From *Lady in the Corner*; 2 Juliana Margolis (*The Newton Boys*); 3 Patrick Swaze, M.Mastroantonio (*Three Wishes*); 4 Vanessa Redgrave (*The Locket*); 5 Halle Berry (*Introducing Dorothy Dandridge*)

1 *The Newton Boys* set; 2 Roma Downey *(A Woman Named Jackie)*; 3, 4 *Sinatra* (with Marcia Gay Harden); 5,6 *Lost in Yonkers* – 5 with producers Caracciolo and Azenberg, 6 with Richard Dreyfuss; 7 with Loretta Young on *Christmas Eve*

1- 6 with Juliana Margolis, Mathew McConahey, Ethan Hawke (*The Newton Boys*); 7 with Michelle Philips (*Assault and Matrimony*); 8 with Charles Bronson (*Murphy's Law*)

1. 1990 Emmy for *The Kennedys of Massachusetts*; 2. 1993 Emmy for *Sinatra* 3. !999 Emmy for *Introducing Dorothy Dandridge* 4. 1993 on the set of *Lost in Yonkers*

Chapter Nine
Don't Be Afraid to Shine

∞ ∞ ∞ ∞

"As we let our light shine, we unconsciously give others permission to do the same. As we are liberated from our own fear, our presence actually liberates others."

Marianne Williamson

I've spent many years not only designing clothes, but also paying attention to the opinions of those who wore them. If something was uncomfortable, I heard about it. I listened to pros and cons as it came to various fabrics and saw firsthand what choices worked better than others.

I have traveled around the world and been exposed to people, styles, trends, fabrics and accessories of every kind. I have seen style disasters and successes beyond what could be imagined. I've enjoyed the benefit of fabrics that can be easily washed, but also suffered the hassle of dealing with some that required special care. I have worked with stars that are very particular and ones who are laid back. Over time I have dressed shapes, sizes and skin tones of every kind.

Because of this, I have always wanted my pieces to be comfortable, to look great, and to be of excellent quality. I prided myself on these factors as a costume designer and of course do so now with my fashion line. Through it all, I have gathered information. I've made mental and written notes, have listened very carefully and obtained feedback. I've seen problems and found solutions. I have paid attention. When developing my own clothing line I was more than prepared to incorporate all this knowledge.

I was able to take what I had learned over many years to create a line of clothing I am proud of. My line has been the result of not only a career working in the field of high end fashion, but extensive research done over many years. An incredibly versatile collection of comfortable, lovely pieces, *Komarov* carries things that are not only stylish, but easy to care for. They are perfect for dressing up or dressing down, wearable for work or play, easy to travel with, adaptable enough to be worn by day…or by night and to look great on you consistently. They are for every woman.

The factors considered in developing *Komarov, Inc.* have always been:

❖ Garments have to be easy to care for.

❖ They have to look great.

❖ There should be versatility in fabric and pattern.

❖ Items should not have to be dry cleaned, but can be washed by hand in a pinch.

❖ Each one should hold its shape.

❖ Wearability is key. Pieces should not wrinkle easily.

❖ They must be easy to pack and no fuss for travel.

❖ Manufacturing will be done in the U.S.A.

❖ Limit a need for alterations by having a forgiving fit.

❖ Availability in small and plus sizes.

❖ They should have a handmade feel and component to them, unlike typical machine made pieces.

❖ Each piece should be unique!

Our fabric is man-made and able to withstand the process of special pleating. We had to find the exact weight, specific fiber and precise temperature to set in these pleats that we designed for our garments and we were very specific in what we wanted. We toiled at length to determine the exact high temperature of close to 400 degrees which would be required to achieve the optimal result. This has allowed us to create a pre-wrinkled clothing option that needs no ironing.

We work with precise patterns involving a combined one and two way pleating. This allows for better stretch ("give") in certain places, either one way or two way stretch as necessary. With my line, I took into consideration that the average person doesn't want to spend great amounts of money or time on alterations. When I think of the amount of money spent on adjustments for films, it's staggering. Besides the obvious expense, getting the right fit can be complicated. Because of this, our pieces are very forgiving. They adapt to your shape easily and are comfortable while still being chic.

It was also very important that our garments could be easily maintained. I didn't want any of our garments to require ironing or dry cleaning, so neither is necessary. They are extremely easy to care for!

It is a tremendous gift to be able to provide gorgeous clothing for today's woman. We work to honor *her*, whoever she is, and we present collections that help her shine. No two pieces in our collections are the same. Each is hand printed and original. This ties in with my belief that no two women wearing them are the same either. Each is unique and special.

Today's woman is on the go. Yes, she goes to all the right functions and is seen at cocktail parties about town, but often that appearance is after a long day. She may regularly put in eight to twelve hours in corporate America or work for herself. Possibly, she is raising a family, traveling extensively and her social calendar is full. If she is still in "mom mode," some of the dates circled on that calendar have more to do with her children's extracurricular activities than hers, so she is very busy.

She rarely has time to care for her wardrobe the way she wants to, even if she has regular help. Again, if she has children, evenings that might have been spent laying out her clothes and planning any alterations are often used for helping with homework. Her down time will usually focus on the family if children are still young, or her husband and not in dealing with her clothes.

The days of apron clad housewives ironing while the roast is in the oven and children happily play in the yard are gone. Today's woman doesn't always have time to spend prepping for what she will wear to the evening's cocktail party, because she is usually busy juggling her many balls in the air that day.

My clothing line is geared towards the woman that wants to look smashing as she goes about her day, but doesn't always have the luxury of time to plan it. She loves to be dressed chic and fashionably, but sometimes needs to be able to do it quickly and with as little hassle as possible. She wants to trust her wardrobe.

She needs clothes that don't wrinkle, apparel that holds up all day. She doesn't want to feel like an unmade bed the way I did years ago at *The Russian Tea Room*. Her goal is to look just as terrific when she goes to meet her husband for drinks with his client (or when he comes to meet hers) as she did when she dropped the children at their school day before heading to her office. Maybe she hopes to show up at a dinner party with her friends looking fresh and relaxed even though she has had a hectic day.

My customers are many different types of women, but they are often socially active. Some have time to leisurely shop. They can devote energy regularly to what they will wear each day. Others have to select a wardrobe online because they just can't find the time to get to *Nordstrom*, *Dillard's*, a specialty shop or boutique. The bottom line for all of them is that they want to look fabulous. They want to appear cool, calm, collected and fashionable. These are the women our company focuses on.

Even the busiest woman has occasions when she absolutely must set aside time to pamper herself. You may have an elegant event to attend where you absolutely want to sparkle. On these days where more energy must be set aside for what you will wear, I recommend having special occasion pieces among your wardrobe. Splurge on them and on the shoes to match. You deserve it.

I have certain items that are exceptional among my wardrobe. They are gorgeous, but a bit fragile. I only wear them once in a while, but when I do, I feel fabulous. I suggest you have those pieces yourself. You never know when you will need to be prepared for an opening night, either your own or someone else's.

Komarov Inc. wants you to be able to reach into the closet and know that whatever you opt for will work beautifully. With my collection in your closet you should never be caught off guard, because our pieces are so versatile. Choosing an outfit can be effortless as long as you have the right choices on your hangers. Whether your days are busy or relaxed, we want you to feel confident with what you have on and look fantastic in it.

When I look back over my career, it is hard to select a favorite time or one experience that was better than another. I am often asked to do so though. The reality is that I've liked them all for different reasons at different times in my life. That's the beauty of life. It has its seasons. What I know for sure is that there is no such thing as having it easy across the board. Just because you have talent, it doesn't mean your work will be effortless. Even the simplest moment can create a challenge. Every film, every project I worked on was both fabulous and difficult depending on the moment.

I think the average person gets caught up with the idea of "stars" and can forget that we are all stars in our own right. That said, I certainly have met and enjoyed working with many talented actors and directors. Some particularly fond memories:

❖ I really liked the time I spent with Neil Simon, Martha Coolidge, Richard Dreyfuss and Mercedes Ruehl during *Lost in Yonkers*.

❖ Memories of *Three Wishes* with Patrick Swayze make me sad, because he passed away soon after that film was made.

❖ Making *Introducing Dorothy Dandridge* was another exciting project with Martha Coolidge, and Halle Berry was fabulous.

❖ I worked on one of the first films of Matthew McConaughey, *The Newton Boys*. This was directed by Richard Linklater and also starred Julianna Margulies and Ethan Hawke.

❖ *The Peacemaker* was the first film of DreamWorks. It was the beginning of George Clooney's career and the film during which I experienced my "green hair" I mentioned in Chapter Four. I had worked with George before on a pilot that didn't go anywhere, so I was happy to see him on that big project. Nicole Kidman, also in the film, was married to Tom Cruise during that time, so all of them were there on the set.

❖ I was in awe working with the fashion icon Loretta Young.

❖ Jack Lemmon, George C. Scott, Vanessa Redgrave, Charles Bronson, Farrah Fawcett and so many more stars come to mind. I am so grateful for having all of the fascinating experiences during my career.

I have so many thoughts, stories, and memories that come to mind when I think about each film, each costume and who wore it. I remember all of it and hold these memories dear.

Today, I like to keep in mind that even the greatest "stars" get up in the morning off the set and dress for the day the way we all do. I sincerely want to encourage women to be the movie star of their own lives. Believe that there's very possibly something more in you just waiting for you to discover for yourself.

I hope that you are willing to be the star of your own life. To select what brings out your best qualities. To shine in front of the camera that is your life. In Hollywood we had plenty of dress rehearsals, but out here, out from behind the camera, this is it. It's show time ladies! Remember that this is your movie and you are not only the star. You are also the director, producer and costume designer. For all of this, I applaud you. I honor you. I sincerely hope to help you shine!

Appendix I
My filmography

Feature Films

The Newton Boys, Twentieth Century-Fox, 1998. Period 1906-26, with Mathew McConahey, Juliana Margolis, Ethan Hawke

The Peacemaker, DreamWorks Distribution, 1997, with George Clooney, Nicole Kidman

Three Wishes, 1995. Period 1950-54, with Patrick Swayze, M. Mastroantonio

My Girl 2, 1994. Period 1970-75, with Jaime Lee Curtis

Lost in Yonkers (by *Neil Simon*), 1993. Period 1944, with Richard Dreyfuss, Mercedes Ruelh

Messenger of Death, 1988, with Charles Bronson

Avenging Angel, 1988, with Charles Bronson

Murphy's Law, 1986, with Charles Bronson

Assassination, 1987, with Charles Bronson and Jill Ireland

Miniseries

Sinatra, 1992. Period 1920-1974. **Won Emmy for Costume Design 1993**

A Woman Named Jackie, 1991. Period 1928-1980. **Emmy Nomination**

Voices Within: The Lives of Truddi Chase, 1990

The Kennedys of Massachusetts, 1990. Period 1906-1960. **Won Emmy for Costume Design** 1990

Roses Are for the Rich, 1987. Period 1950-1985

Peter the Great, 1983-84. Period 1672-1725

TV Movies

The Locket, with Vanessa Redgrave, 2002

Little John, 2002

The Ponder Heart, 2001

The Beast, 2001

The Flamingo Rising, 2001

Introducing Dorothy Dandridge, 1999, with Halle Berry, Klaus Maria Brandauer. **Won Emmy for Costume Design 1999**

Inherit the Wind, with Jack Lemmon and George C. Scott, 1999

Once You Meet a Stranger, 1996

Dalva, 1996

The Client (TV Series), 1995

Secrets, 1995

Lies Before Kisses, with Jaclyn Smith and Ben Cazaro, 1991

The Story Lady, 1991

Bare Essentials, 1991

Coins in the Fountain, with Loni Anderson, 1990

Voices Within: The Lives of Truddi Chase, with Shelley Long, 1990

Spy, 1989

Lady in the Corner, with Loretta Young, her final on-screen appearance, 1989

Final Notice, 1989

Turn Back the Clock, 1989

Take My Daughters, Please, with Lisa Hartman, Bruce Dern, 1988

The Child Saver, with Alfre Woodard, 1988

Assault and Matrimony, 1987

Christmas Eve, with Loretta Young, 1986

Murder: By Reason of Insanity, with Candice Bergen and *Jürgen* Prochnow, 1985

Stage Work

The Cherry Orchard, Pan Andreas Theatre, Los Angeles, 1984
Drama-Logue Award

Appendix II
Samples of the Komarov Fashion

∞ ∞ ∞ ∞

Finally, I would like to present a few images from my fashion line. Hope you like it.

A. Candice Bergen "By Reason of Insanity" B., C., D. Jill Ireland "The Assassination" E. Lisa Hartman "Roses Are For The Rich" F. Loretta Young "Christmas Eve" G. Jill Ireland "The Assassination" H. Alfre Woodard "Child Saver" I. Jill Eikenberry "Assault and Matrimony" J. Hanna Schygulla "Peter The Great" K. Lisa Hartman "Roses Are For The Rich"

A   B   C   D   E

F   G   H   I   J   K

ACKNOWLEDGMENTS

Producing a book is not a solo venture. I want to express my deep gratitude to MaryLois Altmann, Evelina Poghosyan and my husband Boris Komarov for making it possible.